CHRISTIAN
INTERPRETATIONS
OF GENESIS 1

CHRISTIAN ANSWERS TO HARD QUESTIONS

Christian Interpretations of Genesis 1

Christianity and the Role of Philosophy

Creation, Evolution, and Intelligent Design

The Morality of God in the Old Testament

Should You Believe in God?

Was Jesus Really Born of a Virgin?

Peter A. Lillback and Steven T. Huff, Series Editors

CHRISTIAN
INTERPRETATIONS
OF GENESIS 1

VERN S. POYTHRESS

PHILADELPHIA, PENNSYLVANIA

PUBLISHING
P.O. BOX 817 • PHILLIPSBURG • NEW JERSEY 08865-0817

Westminster Seminary Press, LLC, a Pennsylvania Limited Liability Company, is a wholly owned subsidiary of Westminster Theological Seminary.

This work is a co-publication between P&R Publishing and Westminster Seminary Press, LLC.

ISBN: 978-1-59638-686-0 (pbk)

Printed in the United States of America

Library of Congress Cataloging-in-Publication Data

Poythress, Vern S.
  Christian Interpretations of Genesis 1 / Vern S. Poythress. -- First edition
    pages cm. -- (Christian answers to hard questions)
  Includes bibliographical references.
  ISBN 978-1-59638-686-0 (pbk.)
  1. Bible. Genesis I--Criticism, interpretation, etc. 2. Creationism. 3. Bible and science. 4. Religion and science. I. Title. II. Title: Christian Interpretations of Genesis one.
  BS651.P69 2013
  231.7'652--dc23
                2013010219

How do the early chapters of Genesis relate to the claims of modern science? Mainstream science claims that the earth is about 4.5 billion years old and that the universe as a whole is about 14 billion years old. Genesis 1 describes the creation of the world in six days. Is there a contradiction?

People interested in the relationship between science and Genesis have been considering these questions for more than a century.[1] They have come up with not merely one but a whole host of possible explanations. It helps us to be familiar with the possibilities so that we do not too quickly adopt one explanation without considering alternatives.

A Dismissive Approach

To begin with, some people take a dismissive approach to the question. They do not believe that the Bible is really God's own Word, but treat it as merely an ancient human book of religion. According to their view, it is merely mistaken in what it says about the origin of the universe. But we do not think that such an approach does justice to the Bible's claims. So we will consider explanations that attempt to give a positive, respectful interpretation of Genesis 1.

The most obvious division among alternative explanations involves the lengths of the days mentioned in Genesis 1. If the lengths were to be measured, would the days come out the same length as modern twenty-four-hour days? And what are the consequences for our interpretation?

Young-Earth Creationism, with Adjustments to Science

A good number of people, including scientists associated with the Institute for Creation Research, think the earth and the universe are thousands of years old, rather than billions of years old. They understand Genesis 1 to be speaking about twenty-four-hour days. Then what do they say about the claims of modern mainstream science? Some of them undertake to challenge and revise the dating claims made in mainstream science. This approach is often called the *twenty-four-hour-day* theory. But the label is not completely satisfactory, since other theories as well maintain that the days were twenty-four hours long.

The Mature-Creation Theory

Consider next the theory called *mature creation*. It takes its cue from the creation of Adam and Eve. It understands Genesis 2 to be saying that Adam and Eve were created *mature*, rather than growing gradually from babies to adults. If a scientist had been present and had examined Adam and Eve immediately after they were created, he might have estimated their age at twenty-two to twenty-five years, let us say. The age estimate would represent *apparent age* rather than their actual age. In addition, the garden of Eden, as described in Genesis 2:6–9, would have had mature trees. The trees would have had rings in their trunks. By counting rings, a scientist would again arrive at an *apparent age*.

Suppose the scientist examined Adam's eyes and skin and teeth. Would he find incoherent or coherent ages? Would he find that everything came out to about twenty-two to twenty-five years old? Or would he find nine years old for eyes, eighty years old for skin, and thirty years old for teeth? If we believe in the God of the Bible, who is sovereign in creation, we have to say that detailed decisions about how to create Adam are up to God. He can do as he pleases. Nevertheless, one of the options is certainly to produce coherent maturity, that is, coherent appearance of age.

If some things, such as Adam and Eve and trees, were created mature, we may wonder whether the whole universe was created mature. If it was mature, it might in fact be *coherently mature*. If so, the age estimates from modern science, such as 4.5 billion years for the earth and 14 billion years for the universe, are simply coherent instances of apparent age. According to this understanding, the whole universe was created only a few thousand years ago. But it was created with coherent maturity, so that the coherence in scientific explanations of age has a simple explanation.[2]

The Revelatory-Day Theory

Next, the *revelatory-day* theory says that the six days are six days in which God successively *revealed* to the author of Genesis the truths recorded in Genesis 1. The days in question are days organizing the timing of *revelation* rather than the timing of the *acts of creation.*

The Gap Theory

The *gap* theory says that there is a gap in time between Genesis 1:1 and 1:2. Genesis 1:1 describes the original creation by God. Verse 2 describes a subsequent catastrophe. Verses 3–31 describe a subsequent re-creation. This approach was popularized in the notes to the Scofield Bible (1909; revised 1917).[3] According to this view, the results of modern scientific investigation are to be fitted into the time between verses 1 and 3.

The Local-Creation Theory

In a manner similar to the gap theory, the *local-creation* theory says that the original acts of creation take place in Genesis 1:1, while verse 2 describes a cataclysmic devastation in the ancient Near East. The re-creation described in verses 3–31 takes place in a *local area* in the Near East.

The Intermittent-Day Theory

The *intermittent-day* theory says that the days in Genesis 1 are twenty-four hours long, but that there are gaps in time between the days. Much of the creative activity of God takes place within these gaps.

BEFORE WE MOVE ON

✦ What sets the revelatory-day theory apart from other theories discussed thus far? What is distinctive about young-earth creationism?

✦ How might the creation of Adam and Eve lead us to believe that the whole universe was created mature? What is meant by *coherent maturity* versus *incoherent maturity*?

✦ How do the gap theory, local-creation theory, and inter-mittent-day theory incorporate time gaps into the creation account?

The Day-Age Theory

Now we will consider approaches that do not consider the days in Genesis 1 to be necessarily twenty-four hours long. The first such view is the *day-age* theory. The day-age theory says that each "day" in Genesis 1 is a long period of time—it may correspond to whole geologic ages, rather than being merely twenty-four hours long. The day-age theory customarily appeals to the fact that the Hebrew word for *day* (*yom*) can be used in a range of ways:

1. The period of light: "God called the light *Day*" (Gen. 1:5).
2. The period of light and darkness together (twenty-four hours): "Do not eat or drink for three *days*, night or day" (Esth. 4:16).
3. A time of unspecified length that has distinctive character: "In the *day* that the LORD God made the earth and the heavens"

(Gen. 2:4—usually interpreted as referring to the entire time of God's creative work); "The great *day* of the LORD is near" (Zeph. 1:14); "If you faint in the *day* of adversity, your strength is small" (Prov. 24:10); "For the LORD has a *day* of vengeance, a year of recompense for the cause of Zion" (Isa. 34:8).

The day-age theory interprets Genesis 1 as using *day* in the third sense, for a time of unspecified length.

The Analogical-Day Theory

The *analogical-day* theory maintains that the days in Genesis 1 are God's workdays, which are analogous to the workdays of human beings, as indicated in Exodus 20:9–11:

> Six days you shall labor, and do all your work, but the seventh day is a Sabbath . . . . For in six days the LORD made heaven and earth, the sea, and all that is in them, and rested on the seventh day. Therefore the LORD blessed the Sabbath day and made it holy.

The theory claims that this *analogy* between God's work and human work does not imply *identity* in the length of the days. God's workdays are analogous to human workdays, but they need not be exactly the same length as the human days, when measured by modern technical means.

The Framework View

The *framework* view (also called the *framework hypothesis*) says that the days in Genesis 1 are constructed as a *literary framework* to describe God's acts of creation, but that they should not be read as indicating a linear succession of events or a specific amount of measured time.

The Religion-Only Theory

The *religion-only* theory says that Genesis 1 has the purpose only of providing religious teaching about God. It does not supply information that would say anything in potential conflict with modern science.

Nowadays there are several variants of this approach. People may say, for example, that the Bible in general and Genesis 1 in particular answer the questions of "who?" and "why?" while science answers the question "how?" Since the Bible and science are answering different types of questions, apparent conflict arises only from a misunderstanding of the purpose of Genesis 1.

Other people stress the relation of Genesis 1 to stories of origins ("myths") produced in various cultures in the ancient Near East. Because Genesis 1 shows some points of contact with some of these stories, some people may allege that it belongs to the same genre. They may claim that it was never intended to say anything about particular events in space and time, but only to give a general theological or religious statement about the nature of God and his relation to people.

BEFORE WE MOVE ON

+ What are three ways the word *day* (*yom* in Hebrew) is used in Scripture? How might it be used analogically?

+ People who hold to the religion-only theory stress that Genesis 1 answers which two questions? In this view, what question is left to science to answer?

PRINCIPLES FOR EVALUATION

How should we go about sorting through the various theories related to the days of Genesis 1? Are they all equally good? No—some create more difficulties than others. And some may fall prey to mistakes either in evaluating science or in evaluating the meaning of passages in the Bible. We must sift through the good and the bad.

And this sifting is a continual process. A theory that does not look promising at one time may develop more promise as time goes on. Conversely, a theory that looks good at one point in time may run into serious difficulties later on. The gap theory is a case in point. It was popular at one time, and it looked good to a lot of people. But it runs into difficulties with the Hebrew grammar of Genesis 1:1–2. It has few advocates today.

Authority

Our evaluation depends on whom or what we recognize as authorities. No modern scientist can be equally expert in every field of science. Likewise, no modern student of the Bible can be expert in everything that has ever been written about the Bible. And even if people have expert knowledge, they may have personal biases or cultural biases that influence their judgment. We can always ask, "Who says?" and "On what authority does he say it?"

Some people grant almost unlimited authority to modern science. But candid scientists and philosophers of science stress that all scientific results are in principle tentative. Science never reaches a point at which all possible evidence has come in and all possible experiments have been performed. Moreover, scientists never come to a point at which they can truthfully say that they have considered every possible *explanation* of the evidence they already have. In addition, scientists are human, and so they can be tempted to introduce bias either consciously or unconsciously. At the same time, many technological products that depend on modern scientific knowledge demonstrate the impressive power that can come with significant knowledge of how the world works. So the best recipe may be to treat scientific claims with respect but at the same time to be aware of human fallibility. What about the authority of the Bible? Here we have a major dispute. The Bible testifies that it is God's Word; it is God speaking to us in written form. But not everyone accepts this claim. Our view of the Bible obviously makes a big difference in how we go about evaluating the relation of the Bible to modern science.

BEFORE WE MOVE ON

+ As we evaluate different interpretations of Genesis 1, what determines which theories will seem most reasonable to us?

+ What is the best way to treat scientific claims? Why?

The Authority of the Bible

The weighty issue whether the Bible is God's own Word has received extensive discussion.[4] We cannot re-cover all the ground. We can only summarize. Two main classic verses make general statements about the inspiration of the Bible:

All Scripture is *breathed out by God* and profitable for teaching, for reproof, for correction, and for training in righteousness. (2 Tim. 3:16)

For no prophecy was ever produced by the will of man, but *men spoke from God* as they were carried along *by the Holy Spirit.* (2 Peter 1:21)

In addition, 2 Peter indicates that Paul's writings, which belong to the New Testament, have an authority on the same level as the Old Testament: "There are some things in them [Paul's writings] that are hard to understand, which the ignorant and unstable twist to their own destruction, as they do *the other Scriptures*" (2 Peter 3:16).

Jesus testifies in a number of places to the authority of the Old Testament:

> Do not think that I have come to abolish the Law or the Prophets; I have not come to abolish them but to *fulfill them.* For truly, I say to you, until heaven and earth pass away, not an iota, not a dot, will pass from the Law until all is accomplished. (Matt. 5:17–18)

> Scripture cannot be broken. (John 10:35)

In Matthew 19:4–5, Jesus quotes from Genesis 2:24, and indicates that this verse in Genesis is the Word of the One "who created them from the beginning," that is, God himself. Matthew thereby provides an impressive indication that Jesus regarded the Old Testament as God's Word.

A person who wants to be a genuine Christian must be a disciple of Christ, and being a disciple implies submitting to the teaching of Christ the Master. So accepting the Bible as the Word of God is an integral part of Christian faith and living.

The Bible in Relation to Modern Science

Since the Bible is the Word of God, and God is trustworthy, we can trust what the Bible says. The Bible is infallible, while modern scientific claims are fallible. In fact, the Bible offers a positive foundation for science. The Bible indicates that God created and governs all things. His wise and consistent governance is the basis for doing science. Science, rightly understood, endeavors to understand the mind of God and the wisdom of God in governing nature. Hence, science is not to be despised. But it is a human endeavor, and it is fallible.

Since God is consistent with himself, what we find him saying in the Bible is consistent with what he does in creating and governing the world. The difficulty is that since our knowledge is limited, we may not always see *how* the two are consistent.

Since the Bible is infallible, we should give it the preference when conflicts between the Bible and science seem to arise. But not everyone agrees with this principle. Some people in the world around us will make fun of us for following Christ and following the Bible. We should not be surprised, because Christians are called to live a life different from the world: "Do not be conformed to this world, but be transformed by the renewal of your mind, that by testing you may discern what is the will of God" (Rom. 12:2). God has not promised that it will always be easy to avoid compromising with the world, which rejects God's authority and sets up other authorities as supreme.

Interpreting the Bible

In the life of a Christian, the challenges are not always simple. Where the Bible speaks clearly, we can be confident. Even though the Bible is infallible, however, we as *interpreters* of the Bible are not. If there appears to be a conflict between the Bible and science, we have to inspect whether the science has failed because of its fallibility. But we also have to inspect whether we have failed to understand the Bible rightly. Maybe the failings are simple—but maybe they are not. We cannot tell until we have looked.

Many people today think that *only* an interpretation that holds to twenty-four-hour days in Genesis 1 does justice to the divine authority of the Bible. We should respect these people for wanting to make sure that the Bible retains its full authority as the Word of God. At the same time, we need to listen carefully to people who offer alternative views and who also affirm the divine authority of the Bible.

So let us consider the views laid out in the previous section concerning the days of creation. In this short booklet, we cannot hope to offer a full discussion. Readers who want fuller treatment will have to consult full-length books.[5] Here we offer an orientation, so that we may become aware of the main strengths and weaknesses.

BEFORE WE MOVE ON

+ Why must genuine Christians accept the Bible as the Word of God?

+ How does the Bible provide a foundation for science?

+ What are the two reasons why the Bible and science might seem to disagree? What is *never* the reason why?

WEAKER THEORIES

We can quickly pass over some of the weaker options.

The Revelatory-Day Theory

The revelatory-day theory is ingenious, but weak. God did reveal the contents of Genesis 1 to the human author, but Genesis 1 is talking about acts of *creation* rather than acts of *revelation*. No overt evidence in Genesis 1 suggests that the days mark out revelations to Moses rather than periods of creative action. Exodus 20:11 confirms the focus on acts of *creation*: "For in six days the LORD made heaven and earth, the sea, and all that is in them, and rested on the seventh day." It says that in six days God *made* heaven and earth, not that he *revealed* the making of heaven and earth.

The Gap Theory

Next, the gap theory is weak. It runs afoul of the Hebrew grammar in Genesis 1:2. The grammatical sequence in Hebrew—

namely, a conjunction (Hebrew *waw*) plus subject plus perfect verb—is normally used to introduce circumstantial information rather than a new event moving the story forward. Verse 2 means that the earth was without form and void at the time indicated in verse 1, not that it became without form and void in a catastrophe subsequent to verse 1.

The Local-Creation Theory

As does the gap theory, the local-creation theory suffers from serious implausibility. Genesis 1 is the primary account of creation. Psalm 104 and other significant meditations on creation within the Bible reflect back on it. It is not plausible that Genesis 1 would devote only one verse (verse 1) to the main act of creation—which is all-important for a theology of creation. The gap theory and the local-creation theory claim that the whole rest of the chapter discusses only a restoration or a local re-creation, but Genesis 1 gives no clear signal to show that it is no longer discussing the original acts of creation. Ordinary readers therefore naturally (and rightly) read the whole of Genesis 1 as a description of the earliest acts of creation.

The Intermittent-Day Theory

The intermittent-day theory is another ingenious attempt to maintain twenty-four-hour days and still allow for extended periods of time. It does so by putting the extended periods in alleged gaps between the days. It has in its favor the fact that nothing in Genesis 1 specifically says there are no gaps. But neither does Genesis 1 say anything positively about gaps. So we just have inferences from silence, and that is not a firm foundation.

There is an added difficulty. Putting major creative activity of God in the gaps rather than in the days themselves creates tension with the language that we find in Exodus 20:11, where it says that "*in six days* the LORD made heaven and earth." This language appears to place God's work of creation squarely *within* the days and not between them. Moreover, Exodus 20:8–11 makes God's work and rest the pattern for man's work and rest. God's work can properly function as a pattern to imitate only if it, like man's work, occurs *on* the days in question rather than *in between* them.

BEFORE WE MOVE ON

+ How does the wording in Genesis 1 make the revelatory-day theory, gap theory, and intermittent-day theory unlikely?

+ How do passages in the Bible such as Psalm 104 make the local-creation theory unlikely?

The Religion-Only Theory

The religion-only theory is also weak. It has a grain of truth in it, because the Bible customarily does focus on God and his actions. The Bible cares deeply about giving us knowledge of "who" and "why." But it does not totally neglect the question of "how." The two types of questions cannot be neatly separated, precisely because our God is a God who acts in time and space. He works in specific acts of creation in Genesis 1, and he works in history. He calls Abraham, he redeems his people from Egypt, he raises up David as king, and he works climactic redemption through the incarnation, life, death, and resurrection of Christ. His work of redemption and re-creation is *comprehensive* in scope. We do not have the right beforehand to confine him to some narrowly "religious" sphere. He can speak, if he wishes, about any subject that he pleases.

We must indeed respect the main purposes in any portion of Scripture, and interpret the details in the light of the main purposes. But one passage of Scripture may have more than one purpose, and the details always retain their own place. They are not dissolved into thin air merely by an appeal to one main purpose.

We should also observe that Genesis 1–3 is integrated into a larger whole, namely, the book of Genesis. The book of Genesis in turn fits into the Pentateuch, the Five Books of Moses (Genesis–Deuteronomy); and the Pentateuch by God's plan forms the first portion of the canon of Scripture that now includes everything that we have in the Bible today. Genesis as a whole is written about people such as Noah, Abraham, Isaac, Jacob, and Joseph, whom it presents as real people, who lived and died and who went through specific experiences in time and space. References in later parts of the Old Testament and in the New Testament confirm that the Bible regards these people as real people rather than characters in fictional or semifictional stories. Adam, Noah, Abraham, Isaac, and Jacob are listed in Luke 3:23–38 among the ancestors of Christ.

Genesis, of course, is selective in what it records. But it presents the events as events that really did happen. The fact that Genesis 1–3 is integrated into the larger book of Genesis confirms that the first chapters in Genesis are describing events in time and space, things that happened rather than things that are made up.

God wrote Genesis for the people of Israel first of all, but then, as his plan worked out, he speaks also to us and to all the people in the various cultures of the world. He does not address merely people within scientific cultures. So he does not use specialized scientific terminology or delve into details that have been uncovered only by modern science. He speaks in ordinary terms, partly so that no one in any culture may have an excuse to turn away from the true God, partly so that people whose hearts he opens may be instructed about the basic truths of creation.

God "made heaven and earth, the sea, and all that is in them" (Ex. 20:11). We are to recognize him as the one true God. We are to serve him, and not worship creatures. We are to praise him for what we enjoy from the created world. Genesis 1 serves as a foundational instruction about God and his relation to us and the world. Therefore, we should take the whole of Genesis 1, including its details, seriously. The religion-only theory fails to do so by being too simplistic and too restrictive in its expectations for what God may say.

On the other hand, we must avoid the opposite extreme. In modern Western culture, we are so greatly influenced by the interests of science that it is quite possible to overread Genesis as if it were providing detailed scientific information.

The Day-Age Theory

How do we evaluate the day-age theory? The day-age theory in its usual form appeals to the spectrum of meanings for the Hebrew word for *day*. It is correct that there is a range of use. But the use of the word *day* for an unspecified period of time is not the use that most obviously fits Genesis 1. (1) In Genesis 1, the days are numbered and appear to be successive. The numbering fits better with *day* as a human workday. (2) Exodus 20:8–11, in expounding the Sabbath commandment, correlates God's workdays to human workdays. (3) The passages in Genesis 1 describing the days conclude with the expression "and there was evening, and there was morning" (e.g., Gen. 1:5). The mention of evening and morning makes us think most immediately of human workdays.

Together, these observations suggest that the day-age theory needs to be adjusted. If it is adjusted, it gets transformed into the analogical-day theory, to which it is akin. The main difference between the two theories is that the analogical-day theory does not directly appeal to a distinct lexical sense for the word *day*. The analogy in Genesis 1 belongs not to one word, namely, the word *day*, but rather to the whole week, including the evenings and mornings. The time between evening and morning is the evening pause in work, as indicated in Psalm 104:23: "Man goes out to his *work* and to his labor until the *evening*" (note also the mention of the sun setting and darkness in verses 19–20).[6] God pauses between his works from one day to the next. By analogy, man pauses by sleeping and resting in the night. Then he works during the next day. In short, man's workweek is analogically built on the pattern established by God in his initial workweek.

BEFORE WE MOVE ON

+ In what ways is the religion-only theory simplistic and restricting? How does the placement of Genesis 1 in the Scriptures lead to difficulties for the religion-only theory?

+ What are some problems with defining *day* as an unspecified period of time? What simple revision transforms the day-age theory into the analogical-day theory?

THE ANALOGICAL-DAY THEORY

The analogical-day theory has in its favor some further points that need noting. First, the starting point for thinking about analogy is found in the Sabbath commandment in Exodus 20:8–11:

> Remember the Sabbath day, to keep it holy. Six days you shall labor, and do all your work, but the seventh day is a Sabbath to the LORD your God. On it you shall not do any work, you, or your son, or your daughter, your male servant, or your female servant, or your livestock, or the sojourner who is within your gates. For in six days the LORD made heaven and earth, the sea,

and all that is in them, and rested on the seventh day. Therefore the LORD blessed the Sabbath day and made it holy.

The Sabbath commandment points out an analogy between God's pattern of work and rest and man's pattern. The analogical-day theory fully affirms this analogy, but does not deduce that it implies an identity of lengths when times are measured by technical means.

Second, the analogical-day theory applies to the seventh day, the day of rest, as well as to the days of work. Genesis explains God's day of rest as follows:

> Thus the heavens and the earth were finished, and all the host of them. And on the seventh day God finished his work that he had done, and he rested on the seventh day from all his work that he had done. So God blessed the seventh day and made it holy, because on it God rested from all his work that he had done in creation. (Gen. 2:1–3)

The day of rest correlates tightly with God's act of resting "from all his work that he had done in creation" (Gen. 2:3). We know from other Scriptures that God continues to rule the world by his *providence* (e.g., Ps. 103:19; Dan. 4:35; Heb. 1:3). His "rest" does not mean total inactivity, but cessation from his works *of creation*. For example, he is no longer creating new kinds of animals, nor is he creating mankind, because he has done it once and for all. Thus, his rest from the works of *creation* goes on forever. Even the work of creating a new heaven and a new earth (Rev. 21:1) is not an exception, because the consummation belongs to a different order than the first, original creation. The first creation does not need to be created again.

Thus, God's rest from the work of creation is everlasting. By inference, the *day* of God's rest, closely linked with his act of rest, is everlasting. It is not twenty-four hours long. Man's day of rest, commanded in Exodus 20:8–11, can still be twenty-four hours because it is analogical to God's rest. The analogy rather than the identity in length is the salient factor. If analogy belongs to the seventh day, it belongs also to the other six days. So again the salient factor is not the length of time, as measured by a clock of some kind, but rather the kinds of activities that take place during the day.

Third, many cultures, including ancient Israelite culture, live by *social time* rather than clock time. Some cultures do not have mechanical clocks. Rather, time is understood by reference to social activities—talking, eating, socializing, working together. The activities that take place, rather than a clock measurement of length, define the significance of human time. According to this view, God understands this orientation to social time and speaks to it. In the absence of modern technical means for scientific measurement of time, and in the absence of the sun and moon before the fourth day, an orientation involving social time alone makes sense in interpreting Genesis 1.[7] Hence, the days are defined by personal activities, namely, the activities of God's work and rest.

BEFORE WE MOVE ON

+ In Genesis 2, what is God resting from? What does this mean about the *day* of his rest? How does the analogy here then apply to the rest of the creation week?

+ What is *social time*? How does it lend itself to analogy?

THE FRAMEWORK VIEW

The framework view deserves more discussion than we can give here.[8] A few remarks must suffice. The framework view has a kinship with the analogical view, in that both views recognize analogy. In addition, people advocating the framework view have appealed to a certain understanding of Genesis 2:5–6 to justify ignoring the sense of chronological succession that is found in Genesis 1. But there are alternative understandings of Genesis 2:5–6. So it is better to affirm that the signs of literary artistry and elegance in the text in Genesis 1 complement rather than undermine the natural sense of chronological progression. The work of later days builds on the earlier: the lights that are made on the fourth day are put in the expanse that has been made on the second day; the sea creatures made on the fifth day presuppose the sea, which has been made on the third day; and so on.

BEFORE WE MOVE ON

✦ What literary touches do we see in Genesis 1? In what two ways can these be understood?

YOUNG-EARTH CREATIONISM

Consider now young-earth creationism. As we have observed, mature creation, the revelatory-day theory, and a number of other theories maintain that the days in Genesis 1 are twenty-four hours long. But young-earth creationism in its most common form distinguishes itself by disputing many of the dating claims in mainstream science. This dispute constitutes one of its main distinctives. But it also gives rise to difficulties.

Kinds of Dating Techniques

Mainstream science uses more than one technique for dating. The various techniques have different capabilities, but some of the common ones are well established. Here are some of the most well known.

I. *The speed of light.* In astronomy, some dates can be inferred from the speed of light, which determines how long it takes for light to arrive at the earth from distant parts of the universe. The Milky Way galaxy is about a hundred thousand light-years across. Our sun is not located at the very edge of the galaxy, but from our position within the galaxy we can see stars more than thirty thousand light-years away. That means that light takes thirty thousand years to travel from there to us. Astronomers infer that a star that far away must already have existed at least thirty thousand years.

We can also consider galaxies that are neighbors to the Milky Way. The Andromeda galaxy—nearby as galaxies go—is some 2.5 million light-years away, which suggests that the light we now see from it is 2.5 million years old. Other galaxies are still more distant, some up to billions of light-years away. With more distant galaxies, it becomes progressively more difficult to estimate distances accurately, and more assumptions go into the process. But scientists are confident about the distances to nearby galaxies such as the Andromeda galaxy. And even if their estimates were somehow found to be off by a factor of 2, or even by a factor of 10, the results would still involve too much time for young-earth creationism.

2. *Stellar development.* Models for stellar development and nucleocosmochronology are used to estimate the age of stars. The sun comes out at 4.6 billion years old.

3. *Radiometric dating.* In geology, scientists use radiometric dating (also called *radioactive dating*), which estimates the age of rocks by measuring ratios of various radioactive isotopes and their decay products. There are several techniques using different isotopes: radiocarbon, potassium-argon, rubidium-strontium, samarium-neodymium, uranium-thorium-lead.[9] In addition, even before the use of radiometric dating, geologists could come

to rough estimates of age by reasoning about rates of deposition and rates of cooling of molten rock and other processes.

4. *Tree rings.* Counting tree rings (dendrochronology) allows estimates up to the total age of a tree. For unusually long-lived trees, the dates can extend in this way to several thousand years. By carefully correlating between different trees, including those that have already died, one can work back farther. The sequence for Hohenheim oak and pine from central Europe extends to twelve thousand years.[10] A global cross-dating system for tree rings now extends backward twenty-six thousand years.[11]

The results of dating are more impressive when more than one method of dating has been used. Sometimes more than one method of radiometric dating can be applied to the same rock or rock formation. In addition, the age of the solar system can be estimated by radiometric dating of the oldest rocks on earth, by radiometric dating of meteorites, by radiometric dating of moon rocks, by dating the age of the sun from the amount of helium in it (assuming that most of the helium has been produced by fusion of hydrogen within the sun), or by dating the age of the sun by the method of nucleocosmochronology.

Mature creation offers one possible answer to these results in dating, but young-earth creationists usually prefer a different response. Some young-earth creationists are content just to say that something is wrong with the dating methods. Others have gone further and attempted to show flaws in standard methods or offer counterevidence. The amount of argumentation is formidable.[12]

BEFORE WE MOVE ON

✛ What four methods are used for estimating age? As a practical example, how do mainstream scientists estimate the age of the solar system?

✤ How do young-earth creationists distinctively differ in their response to dating from those who hold other Christian interpretations of Genesis 1?

Underlying Assumptions

The criticism offered by young-earth creationists includes at least one valuable point: estimates of age depend on assumptions about physical processes in the past. Mainstream science uses the assumption that at a fundamental level processes in the past are like processes in the present. The speed of light is assumed to be the same in the past as it is today. The decay rates for radioactive elements are assumed to be constant over time. The fundamental processes in stellar development are assumed to be the same over time.[13] All these assumptions can be inspected. Are they in fact valid assumptions?

The Bible shows that God rules the world that he has made. The world is not in the grip of an impersonal, mechanical law, but God rules it personally. The regularities that we see in the world are a reflection of God's personal faithfulness and the consistency of his character.

On the one hand, the consistency of God's character leads to regularities that we can depend on. On the other hand, the personal character of God's rule means that we cannot simply extrapolate backward in time without considering God's purposes. Did God govern the world in the past in the same way as he governs it now?

The unity of God's character and the unity of his purposes for creation suggest an overall unity in his governance. He guarantees consistency in the seasons and in day and night in his promise made to Noah:

> While the earth remains, seedtime and harvest, cold and heat, summer and winter, day and night, shall not cease. (Gen. 8:22)

Exceptions?

But in the Bible we can also see some points in time at which there might be discontinuities in the details of God's providential governance. Miracles, of course, are exceptional in character. But there are also some watershed points in the global character of the world:

1. The time when God initially created the world in Genesis 1:1. At this point there is an absolute discontinuity, because nothing in creation existed beforehand.

2. The time at the end of the six days, when God ceased his work of creation (but not his providential work).

3. The time of the fall. The fall at its heart is an ethical rebellion by Adam and Eve. But it has consequences on the created environment (Gen. 3:17–19; cf. Rom. 8:19–22). The Bible does not indicate how extensive the consequences were. Were the consequences coherent, so that we now observe a *coherently* fallen world?

4. The time of Noah's flood. After the flood, in his promise to Noah in Genesis 8:22, God promises a good measure of continuity. But what about the flood itself? And how much was the world before the flood like or unlike the world after?

5. The time when the new heavens and new earth come, as described in 2 Peter 3:11–13 and Revelation 21:1.

All these pivotal points in time are watersheds at which it is conceivable that God could alter his manner of governing the world. The mature-creation theory can be briefly described as a theory that postulates a radical discontinuity at point 2, the end of the six days of creation.

Mainstream science assumes continuity in the past and in the future as well. And as we have seen from the promise made to Noah, there is indeed a measure of continuity. But it is not absolute. So we need to be circumspect when scientists talk confidently—sometimes overconfidently?—about the far past or the far future.

BEFORE WE MOVE ON

✛ What assumptions do mainstream scientists make about the processes that they observe in nature? From a Christian perspective, why might these assumptions be justified?

✛ Where do we see discontinuity in God's usual governance of the universe?

Caution for Young-Earth Creationism

But caution is also appropriate for young-earth creationism in its interaction with mainstream science. Young-earth creationists themselves need continuity assumptions when they attempt to engage in scientific reasoning. For example, alleged evidence to show change in the measure of the speed of light (perhaps through the general theory of relativity),[14] or change in the rates of radioactive decay, or change affecting still other dating methods, has force only if the argument presupposes *some kind* of continuity. How do we know *which kinds* of continuity to rely on? It is easy to pick out conveniently just those pieces of continuity in physical laws that appear at the moment to support a young earth.[15]

If a well-grounded, unified, global young-earth theory for dating does not yet exist, it does not mean that it may not exist in the future. Science, as we have emphasized, is always tentative. But over the past century the geological and astronomical difficulties for young-earth creationism have grown. People might ask themselves whether the growth in difficulties shows that the starting assumptions of the whole project may be wrong. Do some other approaches to science and Genesis do better justice to the evidence?

CONCLUSION

We end by returning to a point made earlier: it is wise to be aware of several alternatives. Young-earth creationism gets a lot of publicity, both favorable and unfavorable. But there are other positions, among which the analogical-day theory deserves special mention.

It is also worth underlining what we have observed about fallibility. All human theories, whether in mainstream science or in explanations of the days of creation, are fallible. The Word of the Lord remains forever (1 Peter 1:25; cf. Isa. 40:8; Matt. 24:35).

In conclusion

✢ Why is it useful to understand different interpretations of Genesis 1? What pitfalls might we avoid through a basic knowledge of these theories?

✢ Why are none of these theories set in stone?

✢ As we study science and the Scriptures, what are some important points to remember?

NOTES

1. A mid-twentieth-century survey of the options can be found in Bernard Ramm, *The Christian View of Science and Scripture* (Grand Rapids: Eerdmans, 1954), especially 173–249. For an up-to-date discussion, see Vern S. Poythress, *Redeeming Science: A God-Centered Approach* (Wheaton, IL: Crossway, 2006), especially 33–147.

2. Some people have serious objections to mature creation. One such objection is that it might involve apparent deceit on God's part if he made things that looked old but were not. For a discussion of this objection and others, see Poythress, *Redeeming Science*, 117–30.

3. C. I. Scofield, ed., *The Holy Bible Containing the Old and New Testament: Authorized Version*, new and improved ed. (New York: Oxford University Press, 1917), 3.

4. For important discussion, see the Westminster Confession of Faith, chapter 1; Benjamin B. Warfield, *The Inspiration and Authority of the Bible* (Philadelphia: Presbyterian and Reformed, 1948); *The Infallible Word: A Symposium by Members of the Faculty of Westminster Theological Seminary*, 3rd rev. ed. (Philadelphia: Presbyterian and Reformed, 1946); D. A. Carson and John D. Woodbridge, eds., *Scripture and Truth* (Grand Rapids: Zondervan, 1983); John M. Frame, *The Doctrine of the Word of God* (Phillipsburg, NJ: P&R Publishing, 2010).

5. As starting points we can recommend the older work, Ramm, *The Christian View* (1954), and, more recently, Poythress, *Redeeming Science* (2006).

6. C. John Collins, *Genesis 1–4: A Linguistic, Literary, and Theological Commentary* (Phillipsburg, NJ: P&R Publishing, 2006), 77.

7. Modern readers do not usually pause to consider that a discussion about precise *length of time* presupposes a decision about how time will be *measured*. It presupposes a conception of *clock time*, which presupposes clocks, whether mechanical, technical (atomic clocks), or astronomical (perceived movement of the sun). We moderns are so culturally addicted to the presupposition that "real" time must be clock time that we find it difficult to think in terms of social time. In fact, the first three days in Genesis 1 are outside the scope of our narrow cultural biases concerning timekeeping.

8. See Poythress, *Redeeming Science*, 143–47, 341–45.

9. David A. Young and Ralph F. Stearley, *The Bible, Rocks and Time* (Downers Grove, IL: InterVarsity, 2008), 388–443.

10. M. Friedrich, S. Remmele, B. Kromer, J. Hofmann, M. Spurk, K. F. Kaiser, C. Orcel, and M. Küppers, "The 12,460-Year Hohenheim Oak and Pine Tree-Ring Chronology from Central Europe—A Unique Annual Record for Radiocarbon Calibration and Paleoenvironment Reconstructions," *Radiocarbon* 46 (2004): 1111–22, cited in http://en.wikipedia.org/wiki/Dendrochronology, accessed June 28, 2011.

11. Paula J. Reimer, Mike G. L. Baillie, Edouard Bard, Alex Bayliss, J. Warren Beck, Chanda J. H. Bertrand, Paul G. Blackwell, Caitlin E. Buck, George S. Burr, Kirsten B. Cutler, Paul E. Damon, R. Lawrence Edwards, Richard G. Fairbanks, Michael Friedrich, Thomas P. Guilderson, Alan G. Hogg, Konrad Hughen, Bernd Kromer, Gerry McCormac, Sturt Manning, Christopher Bronk Ramsey, Ron W. Reimer, Sabine Remmele, John R. Southon, Minze Stuiver, Sahra Talamo, F. W. Taylor, Johannes van der Plicht, and Constanze E. Weyhenmeyer, "INTCAL04 Terrestrial Radiocarbon Age Calibration, 0–26 cal kyr BP," *Radiocarbon* 46, 3 (2004): 1029–58, cited in http://en.wikipedia.org/wiki/Dendrochronology, accessed June 28, 2011. For an overview on dating methods, see Mike Walker, *Quaternary Dating Methods* (Chichester, England: Wiley, 2005).

12. As a beginning point for astronomy, see the short introduction in Poythress, *Redeeming Science*, 99–105; for geology, see Young and Stearley, *The Bible, Rocks and Time* (old-earth position), and Larry Vardiman, Andrew A. Snelling, and Eugene F. Chaffin, eds., *Radioisotopes and the Age of the Earth: Results of a Young-Earth Creationist Research Initiative* (El Cajon, CA: Institute for Creation Research, 2005).

13. These assumptions are associated with the term *uniformitarianism*. But the term has been used in several senses (see Young and Stearley, *The Bible, Rocks and Time*, 447–74). It should also be noted that scientists try to cross-check their assumptions rather than accepting them blindly. For example, modern experiments have tested whether, within God's current providential order, rates of radioactive decay vary with temperature or pressure.

14. The general theory of relativity postulates a universal constant c for the speed of light in a vacuum, as measured by a nearby observer. But the measurement for distant observers is affected by gravitation.

15. Suppose for the sake of argument that the universe is only six thousand years old. Then how would mainstream science need recasting? Three major alternatives offer themselves: (1) unusual, supernatural action of God at the time of the flood or the fall, or else a change in God's governance at the end of the sixth day of creation, has thrown off mainstream calculations based on continuity of scientific laws; or (2) there is continuity of law, but some major causal influences (such as, for example, a hypothetical preflood "ice canopy") have been left out by the mainstream; or (3) the real laws (for the speed of light or radioactive decay, for example)

are subtly or radically different from what the mainstream has taken them to be.

If we choose alternative 1, it may be impossible to construct a detailed theory for the past, because there are too many ways in which supernatural action can differ from present regularities. If we *do* find regularities nevertheless, the actual accumulation of scientific evidence can move us to the position of mature creation, which simply says that—among millions of possibilities open to God—the regularities happen to be the regularities of coherent maturity.

Within alternative 2, young-earth creationism has already searched about for obvious causal influences. If there is something less obvious, who knows what it is? Until we get clues that narrowly point to one kind of cause, we simply do not know.

Alternative 3 has difficulty because it is speculative. There are too many possible ways in which the existing formulations of laws might need subtle or radical adjustment in the future. It may be wisest to wait to see if, at some time in the future, data of other kinds give us cogent reasons and sufficiently detailed information to make a well-informed, coherent adjustment.

We can also consider *combinations* of these alternatives. For example, some people have suggested that the sun or the garden of Eden or some other structure was created *mature*, but these people then disallow mature creation in other contexts. Or they say that supernatural action of God accounts for one piece of evidence, while adjustment of the laws themselves accounts for other evidence. Such combinations give us so many hypothetical possibilities that real progress toward a coherent, unified global theory is unlikely. Lots of things are theoretically possible—too many to be useful. If this were our situation, we might better say that God did it, but we do not know how. We are better off admitting our limitations.